D1572116

Library of Congress Cataloging-in-Publication Data
Hammerschlag M.D., Carl A.
 Stop Your Sh*t Shoveling
Health, wellness, psychology, mental health, inspiration
eISBN:9781889166407

2022
1931

1

Dedication

To all my patients who shared their lives with me, and trusted that together we would get through the crap and move beyond it.

Acknowledgments

This book would not have happened without:

*Wendy Keller, my beloved agent who said
I could tell a good story in 50 pages
(and maybe one day I could learn to tell one in two minutes.)*

*Steve Kricun and Ryan Acevedo, my computer/
social media consultants, who felt my heart and
created a way to tell my stories around this new fireplace.*

Table of Contents

INTRODUCTION

You know them. You know these people. The ones who tell you their same sob story over and over, perhaps for years, and nothing ever seems to change.

"…And then he cheated on me again, and I know he's not good for me, but I love him/can't leave him/ maybe this time…."

"I hate my job but I can't leave now…"

"It doesn't matter what diet I'm on, I gain it all back, and more."

"He's twenty and not going to school or working. I told him he had to move out, but he won't leave and I can't kick him out."

Those are the Level One Shit Shovelers: the people who occasionally spend time complaining about people/situations/behaviors that give them pain and heartache but always manage to put up with it.

Then there are those on Level Two. These are the people who are getting a PhD (Piled Higher and Deeper) in shoveling. They're the folks you know who endlessly tell you, year after year, about their crummy marriage, traumatic childhood, or the tragedy that happened ten years ago, maybe twenty. You can feel your energy sink when you see their name on your Caller ID.

They're the people who actually believe that moving their shit from one pile to another, from one friend's ear to another, is the same as actually making progress by changing behavior. Somehow magically, talking about it endlessly will turn it into something other than what it is: a big, stinky pile of unresolved issues. Chronic Shit Shovelers continue to spread it around, toss it back and forth, but never do the transformational work required to create lasting change in their lives.

You know these people. Worse, you might even be one of them! Take a deep breath and look in the mirror, because all of us have the capacity to shovel shit at times. When we find ourselves someplace we don't want to be but can't seem to take the risk to move on, we might become shovelers. The good news is that sooner rather than later most of us get it, and we make the necessary changes. We understand that if we keep doing it the way we've done it, we're only going to get to a place we've already been; and if we don't make the change now, then when?

There are people who have the capacity for shoveling shit endlessly. They complain about the suffering/trauma/unfairness of their painful situation, but always seem to hang on to it.

After 40 years as a Yale-trained psychiatrist, I can guarantee you this: there is nothing you can say or do that will stop these shovelers. You can't push anyone into moving forward. They need to see it, believe it for themselves, and lay down their own shovel or they stay stuck.

Some people think the work of psychotherapy is in the shoveling, but it's not. The work of therapy is not just talking about the problem; it's doing something about it. That means putting down the shovel and moving away from the piles. I'll work with someone for a while, but when it becomes clear that the shoveling could be endless, I say, "The more you keep shoveling it, the more you convince me you may be right. You may be locked into your hopeless dilemma, but I'm not an expert in helplessness and can refer you to someone else if you like."

The good news is it doesn't matter how long you've been shoveling shit or how deeply embedded it is in your brain. The brain has the capacity to change itself, a feature known as neuroplasticity. Humans have the ability to create new neural pathways that change the way we see and do things; that's why we can create new endings to our old stories. The human brain is capable of escaping the grip of its old associations. The way it was isn't the way it's got to be in the future.

You really can do this for yourself. You can stop the old pattern and start to deal with the crap that has accumulated in your life, that clogs your field of vision and blocks you from getting what you keep on saying you want but never seem to get. It's not easy to be your own "waste removal technician," as some trash men are now called, but it is possible. If you can lay down your shovel and say, "My work here is done, I'm moving on," it will be an unbelievable relief and maybe even save your life.

Everyone has the capacity to shovel shit occasionally, but we finally get it and make the changes. There are endless scenarios for shoveling shit so I've outlined some repetitive themes to serve as examples…you may recognize yourself.

Chapter 1
Why do we do it?

I saw a baby in a stroller one afternoon. He was wearing a T-shirt that simply said, "Spit happens." While that's surely true for babies, as we grow and interact with our parents and our world, a whole lot more than spit happens. In fact, in most people's lives, the "spit" hits the fan. We learn what to watch out for, what gives us pain, what gives us pleasure, and who helps us when we're hurt or sad. Sometimes we hang on to the painful things with such intensity that we keep looking at the world through the eyes of our early childhood.

Figuring out how to clean out the shit is what we learn as we grow up and becomes our duty when we reach adulthood. Many people can't do it. In my opinion, every human being over 18—legal adulthood—is 100% responsible for cleaning up the shit in their lives and learning how to be careful not to step in it again.

Here's a simple test to help you figure out if YOU could perhaps be your own best expert shit shoveler.

You Are A Shit Shoveler If...

☐ You have complained about the exact same behavior in another person – your mate, your child, your parent, or your boss – more than twice in the last week.

☐ There are times when you're just so freakin' exhausted you say, "I just can't deal with this anymore" and give up – and give in – to any compulsive behavior. (Alcohol, drugs, food, shopping, sex, too much TV watching, etc.)

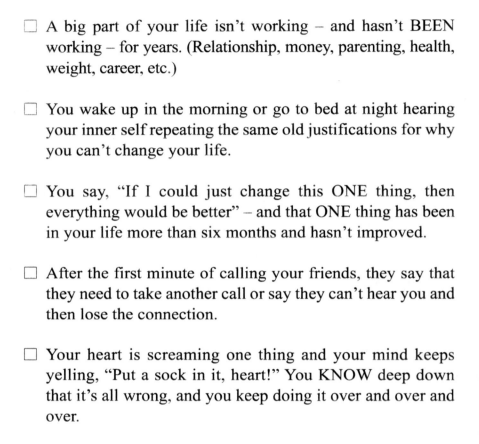

☐ A big part of your life isn't working – and hasn't BEEN working – for years. (Relationship, money, parenting, health, weight, career, etc.)

☐ You wake up in the morning or go to bed at night hearing your inner self repeating the same old justifications for why you can't change your life.

☐ You say, "If I could just change this ONE thing, then everything would be better" – and that ONE thing has been in your life more than six months and hasn't improved.

☐ After the first minute of calling your friends, they say that they need to take another call or say they can't hear you and then lose the connection.

☐ Your heart is screaming one thing and your mind keeps yelling, "Put a sock in it, heart!" You KNOW deep down that it's all wrong, and you keep doing it over and over and over.

If you said, "That's me" to the majority of these questions, then you're a serious shit shoveler. This does not mean there is no hope. It DOES mean you are going to have to get tough with yourself, take a hard look at your ridiculous repetitive behavior, and prepare yourself to try something new. Why something new? Because it should be obvious by now that what you've been doing is getting no positive results. Something new has at least the probability – although not the certainty – of helping you make things better for yourself.

The great news is that the brain has the capacity to change itself, and you can learn new behaviors. Brain scientists tell us that the brain is always changing itself; this phenomenon is called neuroplasticity, as mentioned before. The paradox of neuroplasticity, however, is that constant repetition can prevent changes from occurring. When you keep using the same neural pathways, your thoughts and behaviors travel through well-worn brain routes that become deeply rutted and more unchangeable. That's why habitual thoughts and actions tend to become self-perpetuating.

Bad habits can take over our brain maps because every time we repeat the behavior, it claims more control of the brain and prevents the use of that space for establishing new habits. It's best if you can get it right early on, because bad habits always have a competitive advantage. Like everything else in life…it's use it or lose it. Dr. Norman Doidge says it beautifully in his remarkably readable book on neuroplasticity, *The Brain That Changes Itself* "It's hard to learn a new language when you are tyrannized by the mother tongue." This means the longer you've heard the messages and learned the behaviors in the language you know best, the more difficult it is to unlearn it.

You can do it, however; your mind can create detours that will take you off the old behavioral highway. Here's an example:

Sall, a fifty-ish year old businesswoman who suffered from panic attacks. The kind of terror that came from not being able to breathe, crushing chest pain, resulting in her calling 911. The paramedics would take her to an emergency room, sometimes she was admitted, but the tests were always negative.

I'd seen Sally over the years, and she understood that her panic attacks were likely to occur when she was feeling alone and vulnerable. She knew they stemmed from fears about being abandoned that lingered from childhood. As a five year old, she remembered being taken to the ER for what were thought to be asthma attacks. These episodes were often triggered when her parents left her in the care of a nanny when they went on long business trips. Sally understood the unconscious dynamics of her behavior, but having insight didn't change it. If she sustained a significant loss (two husbands/ lovers/ business setbacks), she'd find herself trapped on the panic highway.

Insight into a problem doesn't necessarily change the behavior. To change behavior, you must give your brain a new set of instructions. You have to create detours on the highway of destructive habits. The way to do that is by altering your consciousness and learning to see the familiar from a new perspective.

As a species, humans have been altering their consciousness since the beginning of time. Ancient healers might drum, pray and light incense, yogis use breathing to induce meditative states, monks chant, dervishes dance; these are all trance states that allow the brain to see what you know in new ways. My favorite detours utilize guided imagery, chants, myths, and rituals.

I told Sally that if she were willing, I would give her the instruments to perform a ceremonial cleansing of the past and coming into the present moment. It was a ritual she'd seen me use many times before, it's how I begin my sessions…

...This fragrant smoke that I use when we began which was intended to take whatever cosmic dust still clings to us from where ever we were and what ever we were doing before this moment, and come together to focus on being here. This smoke gives color and smell to our words and allows us to watch them move beyond this place, and carry our dreams to the heavens...

I gave Sally some cedar and a feather, both of which came with a story, and suggested she create a sacred space in her home, a place she felt good where she could place these instruments on a personal altar, perhaps with other symbols/objects/ that made her feel surrounded by a loving energy.

I told her that if she started feeling her fear and anxiety escalating, to go to her sacred space, sit down, light the cedar, and brush the smoke all over her with the feather. The smell would remind her of the forest and trees, many things that were sustaining connections would surround her, including my voice. She might hear me speaking or singing as she breathed in the sacred smoke.

I told her... *Even when you feel alone, you are not alone, you are surrounded by living reminders who will help you on this road of life, and by the time it takes you to perform this ritual you will have created a new brain brain pathway.*

Sally did it once, and then again and again, until she never again called 911.

Chapter 2
How do we learn to stop doing it?

Shit shoveling is the mechanism for avoiding facing our fears. If you could stand still long enough and look your "fear monster" in the eye, it would actually grow smaller – and smaller means manageable, conquerable, and possible. If you've ever seen an ant in a microscope, you know they are terrifying-looking creatures, but when is the last time you felt terrified by an ant? You've probably *eaten* ants at picnics and not even known it!

None of us can outrun our fears; they always seem to catch up with us. We have a choice of hiding under our piles or getting unstuck and moving on. Sooner or later, we either choose to face our fears, or don't and hide from them under our pile of shit.

There is something oddly comforting about the shoveling, because we know it so well. Even if the shit causes endless misery, PhD shovelers can always find more reasons to stay stuck rather than take a step forward. When that happens we minimize our dreams and magnify our fears.

A 60-year-old man with non-alcoholic cirrhosis of the liver for 10 years had recently been discovered to have cancer of the liver. However, they found it too late for Steve to be a candidate for transplant surgery. Steve was angry at the doctors for having missed it. He was angry at himself for not being more vigilant, and he was feeling a growing anxiety about facing the end of his life. He came to see me hoping I would take him to see an Indian medicine man to perform a healing ceremony.

We found another way of doing some deep trance work. On one journey into his unconscious, he found himself sitting in front of a cave around a fireplace with Neanderthals. They made room for him but he couldn't understand a word they were saying. After a while, one of them, the Chief or Shaman, stood up and motioned for Steve to join him and go into the cave. He went to him, took a torch from his hand, and followed him.

On the cave walls, Steve saw pictures of animals and many hand prints. He put his own hand into one of them, and when the shaman saw Steve do it, he motioned for him to put his hand on the blank wall. Steve did as he was told, and the shaman spit a white, chalky liquid out of his mouth that outlined his hand on the wall. When Steve stepped away to look at his handprint, he saw the ends of his fingers beckoning for him to come closer. When he did so, he saw the faces of his grandchildren on his fingertips. At that moment, he was overwhelmed by a sense of all encompassing peace and felt the fear monster of anxiety lift from his shoulders.

Let's be clear. All of us get afraid sometimes, and we find a way to face the monster with little shoveling. Everybody shovels shit, maybe only for days, weeks, or sometimes months, but it might be years. It doesn't matter how well-educated, competent, and productive you are, shit happens.

For example, Dr. Mehmet Oz, America's most famous medical doctor: a warm, open, believable, and knowledgeable soul whom I like and respect, when faced with a recent cancer scare, started shoveling too. He told his story in the cover of *Time Magazine* (June 13, 2011).

Dr. Oz announced publicly at his 50th birthday party that he was scheduling his first colonoscopy. This is something he routinely counsels his patients to do, and he was not afraid. After all, he had nothing to fear. He ate well, exercised regularly, was working at a job he loved, and his stressors were minimal. He went through the uncomfortable prepping ritual to cleanse his bowels, except he ate some lentils when he should have been fasting. At the examination, his gastroenterologist found a polyp, which turned out to be pre-cancerous. His doctor, who was also a personal friend, scolded him about the lentils because they partially obscured portions of his colon. He wanted to repeat it, giving Dr. Oz a three-month window to reschedule the procedure.

Remarkably Dr. Oz stalled, even after his friend called to remind him. He shoveled because in his head he knew that even with his pre-cancerous polyp, people like him had only a 5% chance of developing colon cancer. But in his heart, he knew that he dreaded getting a bad diagnosis, and he wasn't ready for the complications that would bring to his life. Dr. Oz said it wasn't that he believed he was immune from disease or death, but until now, it always seemed so remote. His pre-cancerous polyp forced him to recognize that he could be out of control of his own life.

When we see the passage into the unknown, all of us start shoveling. Dr. Oz shoveled for nine months before he faced his fears and went back for the follow-up. This time he followed the instructions to the letter. They found another polyp in one of those obscured places that turned out not to be pre-cancerous. Still, Dr. Oz knows that he has to be careful, has to show up for periodic testing – and he will do it.

He is a gifted physician and role model who reminds us that to stop shoveling, we must find the courage to show up in our own lives.

Chapter Three
Sh*t Shoveling in Relationships

Sara was a 40-year-old divorced woman with a teenage son. A highly regarded professional in the prime of her career, she was looking for a long-term relationship, not necessarily marriage but a companion. Her great shoveling talent was her ability to keep falling for men who were always unavailable to her. They were attractive, bright, talented men, who were always on the brink of success in their job and relationship but then always managed to drop out and move on.

The beginnings were always great. They were compatible in every area, but they lasted an average of less than a year. First, there would be missed dates for which excuses were made or a sickness before vacations. Then she'd find out that he was either lying or intentionally withholding from her. Even when she could feel them distancing themselves, she would put up with it. After he left, she'd rage at herself for putting up with it. I saw Sara after one of those breakups when she became so despairing that she wanted to give up entirely.

Sara told me she was raised in a religious cult in which women were inferior and subject to the rules of men. Women sat in the back of community meetings, were not called upon to speak, had little education, married young, and bore children. Sara was a bright, curious child who wanted to go to college. When she decided to get an education, the community not only refused to support her, they shamed and rejected her.

She married young, divorced young, and was left as the sole supporter of her son. She worked while putting herself through college and graduate school and became a marketing whiz. She never remarried but had lots of boyfriends.

Sara was a creative, intelligent, beautiful woman who knew she could get what she wanted if she put her mind to it, but why didn't it happen with men? First, we talked about her expectations of men, and what she was getting out of her repetitive shit shoveling behavior.

I got into her face and told her that if she had to be good enough in a man's eyes in order to feel good about herself, she may never feel good. She picked men who were unavailable and punished herself again and again. She was angry at men and raged against the humiliation and rejection she experienced, but she also raged against herself for continuing to repeat the behavior.

Sara had a choice to make: unlearn the old messages, de-frag her brain hardware and decide she was good enough to be in a relationship other than as an abused little girl. That old story was an enemy she carried within that set her up to find abusive, controlling men.

I learned this profound story about the enemy within when I was in Africa staying at a tent encampment on the Serengeti. I'd befriended Joseph, a Masai warrior who was employed by the hotel as the tribal cultural representative. Joseph guided tours, gave lectures, and could speak three African languages, English, and some Japanese. We had talked some, and he knew I was a psychiatrist who had worked with tribal people. The evening before our departure date was New Years Eve, and Joseph asked if he could speak to me about a problem he was facing. He told me this story. It was Joseph's birthright as the eldest son to become the chief of his tribe, but after his education and being exposed to tourists from around the world, he no longer wanted to live in his village in a dung hut. He wanted to pick out his own wife, and choose one who had not been ritually circumcised. His father, the current tribal chief, told him if he did that he would not inherit the chiefdom. Joseph prided himself on being a Masai warrior, and he did not want to disappoint his father, so he decided not to bring the subject up again.

Joseph wanted to know if Native Americans had similar problems with cultural changes. I told him yes, and that in my experience it was indeed possible to be a traditional Masai warrior and still enjoy taking hot showers. He knew that sooner or later he had to tell his father what he was feeling, and I encouraged him not to hide from it. His father probably already knew his dilemma; after all, he had helped shape the man he was now. His father had chosen him to be the bridge person between his tribe and this new world, which meant not only teaching what he knew but also learning ways that moved him beyond the boundaries of his village. If he could face his father and share his truth, his guilt and misery would lessen.

Before leaving the next morning, Joseph showed up at our tent. I didn't recognize him at first; walking toward me was not a Masai warrior dressed in traditional clothes and hairdo. Instead, there was a young man in khaki pants, a sport shirt, and a crew cut. When he got closer, I saw it was Joseph. He said that to welcome this New Year he was going to speak to his father. He wanted to thank me for helping him come to this decision and wanted to give me something. He reached out and gave me his ornately carved Masai warrior's club and said, "I have come to peace with the truth inside me and will tell my father I will not become tribal chief, but I will always be the tribal chief's son." He handed me a note, which I later read. It said, "Thank you for helping me better understand this teaching from my people – 'If there is no enemy within, the enemy outside can do you no harm.'"

I repeated this saying to Sara, "If there is no enemy within, the enemy outside can do you no harm." Then I gave her two tasks. The first was that she couldn't go out with anybody without asking herself, "What do I really want going into this?" The second was that she could only go out with men that she previously would not have considered going out with. She had to look at something other than his face and body.

If she found herself looking at the man's face, I told her to look down to his chest and imagine she could see into his heart. If she could trust what she saw, she could go out with him again. At the end of a month, we would see each other again and look at what was happening. It took a few months, but Sara learned how to connect with men at a different level. Now she opened the window of her heart to someone else whose window was also open, and this abused little girl's shell opened up and let the proud woman emerge.

Sara found a man whom she would never previously have ever considered dating. He was short, stocky, and balding, but he did have a great sense of humor, was bright, the CIO of a Fortune 500 company, and divorced with shared custodial responsibility for two adolescent sons. It wasn't love at first sight, but she respected him and he was smitten with her. After second, third, and fourth sightings, it became a committed loving relationship.

Pete is a 48-year-old corporate attorney who in his spare time does volunteer work for homeless veterans. Mary is a cosmetic dentist who in her spare time organizes high society functions. Pete and Mary have been married for 15 years, but now sleep in separate bedrooms and have not had sex for the last five. Pete stays because of the children. His daughters, Amanda, age 13, and Serena, age 10, are the light of his life. He will never leave them.

Pete came to see me after discovering his wife was having an affair. In spite of his pain and anger, he was still not sure he wanted to leave the marriage, wondering what difference it should make with whomever she slept. The girls provided the meaning and purpose of his life.

Pete's sense of right and wrong were learned early on. He was the first-born son in a religious Catholic family and had learned about sin, guilt, and shame. Pete understood the sacred obligation to sacrifice one's own needs to a greater cause; for him to ask directly to have his needs met was to be selfish.

The pain and anger he felt was nothing compared to the loss of seeing his beloved daughters every day. Pete wondered what difference it made who she slept with anyway? He told himself he could surely stay until they got through high school.
Talking with me may have softened him a bit to opening himself to other ways of seeing, but he was still shit shoveling eight months later. Then he met a woman at his local gym who was running on the treadmill next to him. Their casual conversation developed into a friendship. Then he found

himself dreaming about her and getting excited. He punished himself for those thoughts but negotiated a peace with it as long as he never touched her. That lasted another three months until he kissed her.

You know the rest of the story. They fell in love, and that's when he finally believed that the way it was, wasn't the only way it could be and created a new ending to his old story. He married this woman and negotiated a shared custodial relationship for the children.

Everybody knows some variation of this shit shoveling theme – husbands and wives who stay together for the sake of the children. Although, it's never been clear to me what it's doing for the children other than teaching them a dysfunctional model of what relationships ought to be about. It would be so much better to show your children your love and commitment to them, even if you are no longer committed to each other. Parents could then teach a model of loving that included forgiveness, respect for differences, living in truth, and pursuing happiness as a goal and not a leftover.

Chapter Four
Sh*t Shoveling at Work

Paul was a 49-year-old married, successful businessman who spent the last 25 years in his father-in-law's paint business growing increasingly unhappy. He graduated from college when he was 23 with a pregnant wife and a degree in land conservation and water management. His father-in-law made him a job offer that came with good benefits, and it made sense at the time and was hard to refuse. He bought a house near his wife's parents. Life was beautiful, and he was happy. The business thrived, and with Paul's administrative talents, the business expanded. By the time he was 32 years old, Paul had three children, was a little league baseball coach, and the company president.

At 40, the business no longer made him so happy, and he needed to look forward to a bottle of wine at the end of the day. His joy came from exploring "green technology" and developing an idea to make deserts bloom based on traditional Native American dry-farming techniques.

He wanted to get out of the paint business and create a technology start-up company. Alas, he had a ski cabin in Arrowhead and a beach house in Coronado, which he didn't want to give up. Over the next nine years, he began looking forward to two bottles of wine every night, and on his way to work one Monday morning, he doubled over with chest pain and was hospitalized with a heart attack and needed bypass surgery.

During his convalescence, his cardiologist suggested he come to see me if he was serious about changing his behavior. Paul knew he was shoveling shit, and that if he kept drinking and stressing, he'd die with a broken heart. If he wanted to heal his heart then today might be the first day he needed to pay attention to what his heart was telling him instead of his head.

Six months after his heart attack, Paul sold his business and started a green technology company.

This is how it often works: some disaster befalls us, forces us to step back from the pile we've been shoveling, and gets us to look at our familiar from another perspective. We finally say, "Enough! I'm putting my shovel down."

My friend Jeff is now a world-class sculptor. In his former life, he was a medical social worker. Jeff worked at the county hospital, and his specialty was working with abused kids. He was wonderful with them. They saw in him a kindness that would not betray them. He stayed in this difficult job for 15 years, but when the county needed to make budget cuts, it meant larger caseloads and less support, the classic set-up for burnout.

Jeff wanted to leave and pursue his passion, which was woodworking. He was a master craftsman who created original pieces of furniture. But with a wife and two kids that he supported on a modest income with good retirement and health benefits, he stuck it out.

In his spare time, Jeff replenished his soul in his basement workshop where he created very contemporary sculptured chairs and tables that he sold in design galleries. He couldn't produce enough to give up his full time job, so he dabbled at it and made do. Until one day, he almost bled to death from a gastric ulcer.

Jeff knew that if he stopped the stressors maybe he would stay well. He knew where the stress was, and he knew what he needed to do. He wanted to quit his job. His wife said she was ready to teach school again, and they would surely get by. They did it, and he did better than get by; he became a locally and nationally recognized artist.

You don't have to have a near-death experience to stop shoveling; you just have to find a new way of listening to what your beautiful heart is singing.

Chapter Five
Sh*t Shoveling with Body Image

Sherry is an attractive, full-figured, cosmetologist who has been chubby since childhood. Even when she was at her lightest weight, she thought she was too fat. If her weight bloomed 25 pounds over her ideal weight, she cycled through the latest diets and exercise fads, would lose the pounds, and then regain them, sometimes adding even more.

For anyone who has ever struggled with being overweight, this is a depressingly familiar story. It doesn't matter what you've done, somehow the weight fluctuation continues and the cycle goes on. Losing weight for a short time is easier than maintaining a good weight. I'm not talking about perfection, just a good weight for your height and build.

Real, transformational change only comes from changing your attitude. It's not just the food and exercise; everybody knows about those necessary lifestyle changes, like eating a healthy, vegetable-rich, low-carbohydrate diet, avoiding processed foods, and giving up the cultural tradition of "carby" munchies and sweet treats.

Keeping weight off is all about developing a new attitude. To stay slim, you need to develop new skill sets only a few of which have anything to do with food and fitness. It's easy to learn how to eat better and stay active, but success has much more to do with your brain not your body. If you want to stay slim, you have to stay positive and regularly give yourself praise, pep talks, and back pats for staying on track. Every day you need to tell yourself, "Great job!" If you want to stay slim, you need to develop a new attitude; you have to get a thrill from standing on the bathroom scale at least once a week, and every pound you lose ought to be greeted with fist-pumping joy as if you just won the lottery. This attitude is a built-in mechanism to keep the buzz going. Give yourself credit for sticking with the program and be tolerant if you gain a couple pounds. What matters most is not to get down on yourself and into the old dysfunctional habits.

If you get off the track, make a u-turn and get back on. It's not easy to lose weight, and it may not happen as fast as you'd like it to. You will have bad days, but 26 out of 30 is a good month. It's not about perfection; it's about moderation and consistency.

Why don't you do it? Because you get more from shoveling it than changing it. That's right. As hard as you work, if you keep snapping back to a weight that makes you sad, you have to consider, WHY? What are you getting out of it?

Here's what I suggest to help you get to the real why.

Answer these questions on a sheet of paper in a private space. Continue answering it until you really can't think of one more thing, and then add ten more. Ideally, you'll have at least 25-30 answers off the top of your head for each question. It doesn't matter if they sound silly or crazy – don't censor yourself. Just let your heart do the talking for a few minutes. Go!

1. The reason I like being overweight is….

2. I feel _____ when I am a little bit chubby.

3. Food to me is like…..

4. If someone asked my advice, I'd tell them this about why diets don't work:

If you're getting enough out of doing what you've always done, then I suggest you stop the shoveling, sit down, smell the roses, and find a way to feel good about who and where you are. But if you're unhappy with the way you look, then the only way to move beyond food is to make a transformational change in attitude. Do it, and you will develop the capacity of persistence and patience.

What does it take to succeed? All those things we learned to read as kids in *The Little Engine That Could* and *The Tortoise and the Hare*; if you hang in there, you will succeed. Here, it is to eat better, exercise regularly, and enjoy looking at who you are.

Speaking about enjoying looking at yourself, let's talk about body image and cosmetic surgery. Do you know what the number one gift request is for girls who are graduating high school? Breast augmentation surgery. The most beautiful breasts are large, perky, and untouched by gravity. Who decides what the most beautiful breasts look like, or that to be attractive your pubic area has to be hairless? Or the newest surgical craze: labial enhancement surgery. In less than two hours as an outpatient surgical procedure that costs anywhere from $3500-$8000, plastic surgeons are reshaping women's labia, to make them more beautiful, smooth, and firm.

As soon as women bear children, their labia may seem ragged

and droopy. Women tell their doctors that they are uncomfortable in tight pants, thongs, or riding bicycles. Their surgeons tell them there is a procedure the beauty industry calls "vaginal rejuvenation."

I'll let you in on a secret, most heterosexual men don't care whether the labia are indented, drooping, beaded, pierced, or tattooed. If they are that close, they just want to get in. If you see yourself as lovable, and love your sex life, you don't need "vaginal rejuvenation." A far safer and more effective program to rejuvenate your vagina is to exercise it more.

Where does this craze come from? The plastic surgeons surely don't mind sculpting anything, but the real drive comes from aggressive marketing campaigns by the fashion industry, and the over-exposure of bare genitalia courtesy of the pornography industry.

Flab and pubic hair have also gotten a bad name. Adult women will make monthly appointments, at a cost anywhere from $35 to $200, to have their pubic hair waxed and painfully ripped out. When a special bikini wax is applied to the pubic area, it dries for 15 to 30 minutes and then is torn off in what most women describe as excruciating pain. There is no woman who looks forward to them, and as a matter of fact, most prepare themselves for the ordeal by taking painkillers and then applying expensive lotions afterward to sooth their panicked pubes.

And this is not just about women, because men are surely making appointments to have their pec's enhanced, their butts rounded, and bodies waxed. But as a general rule, men spend less time in front of mirrors. And when they do, it's not a microscopic exam, twisting and turning until they can spot an imperfection. Men take a quick look, make some minor straightening, and decide it'll do, and it's all they want to know.

The question for all is, how much pain, how much cosmetic surgery are you willing to put up with before you decide to stop shoveling somebody else's sense of perfection? You'll save a lot of money, pain, and heartache if you can see yourself as beautiful and whole just as you are.

Chapter Six
Sh*t Shoveling With Parents

Paula is a middle-aged woman who lives in the same town as her 85-year-old mother to whom she is close. Her mother still lives in the house Paula grew up in 50 years ago. Her mother cooks for herself, drives her own car, plays cards with friends, and goes to church, but her health is declining. With chronic congestive heart failure, her mother can no longer climb the stairs at home because she gets short of breath. Her eyesight is slowly deteriorating, and soon she will no longer be able to drive.

Paula visits her almost every day. She has spoken to her about moving into a residential community where she could live independently and get more care if she required it in the future. The subject is always cut short when her mother says, "I'm never leaving my house while I can still breathe."

After two years of daily visits and her mother's escalating needs, Paula came to see me for her depression. We talked, and Paula understood the piles she was shoveling. On one hand, she wished to honor her mother's freedom and dignity. However, on the other, she felt her mother's needs were more than she could handle. Feeling guilty about it, she was unable to tell her mother directly that she didn't want to do it this way anymore. I recommended Paula take a walk through the botanical garden, which happens to have a butterfly aviary on its grounds. Her mother loved to visit the place, sit on a bench, and watch the hundreds of species do their colorful dance. I told her to visit the place, sit amongst them, and talk to them about the crisis she was facing.

Paula went, sat on a bench, and became entranced watching the butterflies in their hypnotic dance. One butterfly stayed for a long time, fluttering its wings, and Paula thought it was welcoming her. She began a conversation with it. She spoke of her sadness at watching her mother decline and her inability to get her mother to move to a more supportive environment. Paula said she dreaded going to visit the house, and then began to cry. That's when Paula thought she heard the butterfly's wings speak to her and say, "When there is no joy in it, you will only bring resentment."

That week, Paula told her mother the truth. She told her mother that she loved her dearly but could no longer come to see her as often as she had. If she chose to stay in the house, she would need a caretaker to come in, or she could choose to go to a retirement community with medical facilities if she ever needed them. Paula would help her make whatever choice she decided and would visit her wherever she chose to live. They visited retirement homes with and without options for extended care, and they interviewed home health agencies. As soon as Paula got clear and put her shovel down, her mother finally moved to a place she grew to really like.

It works the other way too – parents staying in the family home and the kids refusing to leave. Kids in their 20s and even into their 30s are living at home. I know part of it is surely that these economic times are difficult, but it's more than unemployment and tight money. Ours is becoming a culture of residential adolescence.

I'm not talking about the young people who've lost jobs and take on household duties when they move in, contribute rent, go to school, and even help support their parents. I'm talking about parents who let their kids move in without any expectation of helping out. Some parents are making it too easy for their adult kids to hang around and are finding all kinds of shit shoveling reasons to accept it.

How do you know when it's time to put your shovel down? If you're paying somebody to mow your lawn while you're unemployed, 30-year-old, out-of-school son and his girlfriend are hanging out in his (now "their") room, and you feel like walking in and strangling him, maybe it's time. Maybe it's time to tell him this is not a motel with cable, Internet services, laundry, and a free parking space. May it's time to say, "Grow up and get any kind of job because you're out at the end of the month."

Goethe said that the only things we have to give our kids are roots and wings, and it still holds true. If you keep them in the nest too long, they will never learn to fly.

Chapter Seven
Sh*t Shoveling With Children

The most significant shit shoveling story in modern American life is that if your kids are having a hard time staying focused, are inattentive, overactive, easily distractible, doing poorly in school, or not listening to their parents, they could be suffering from Attention Deficit Disorder (ADD) or Attention Deficit Hyperactivity Disorder (ADHD) and need to be medicated. Parents are buying this story even though they are aware that the long term effects of these drugs on kids is unknown, and even when they don't work, keep giving it to them because doctors tell them the symptoms might get worse.

Forty years ago this diagnosis didn't exist, but psychiatrists working hand-in-hand with pharmaceutical companies have created an epidemic of mental illness by defining unacceptable behaviors as "diseases." In the last 10 years, ADD/ADHD has reached epidemic proportions largely with the discovery of drugs to treat these symptoms. One out of every six children in America is now labeled with a developmental disability, due almost entirely to a rise in the diagnosis of attention deficit disorders.

This is the story being told by psychiatric researchers and pharmaceutical companies; these kids have a biological dysfunction, their brains may be smaller in those areas controlling cognitive (thinking) and motor skills. How much smaller these regions of the brain have to be before they cause the symptoms is not clear. Unlike other medical diseases, we have no idea what causes it or how it's transmitted because it can't be well defined. ADD/ADHD is often confused with other conditions like anxiety, depression, and learning disabilities, so the label is applied indiscriminately.

In spite of these serious limitations, the preferred story is still to treat this poorly defined dysfunction with potent drugs. We must stop shoveling this story; every kid who's having a hard time sitting still or gets distracted from what he or she is doing when the music of a favorite cartoon comes on screen is NOT suffering from ADD/ADHD. One out of every six children in this country is **NOT** suffering from a mental disability. I see ADD as a trait not a disability and when it's managed properly it can be a huge asset in one's life. People with these traits are often creative, intuitive, persistent and sensitive. The problematic aspects can be improved by treatment other than drugs. Child psychiatrist Edward Hallowell, co-author of *Driven to Distraction: Recognizing and Coping With Attention Deficit Disorder* says, "having ADD is like having a powerful race car for a brain but with only bicycle brakes. Treating ADD is like strengthening your brakes."

The real crisis is that we have legitimized these unacceptable behaviors by declaring them diseases. Giving the symptoms a name implies that we know what we're dealing with and how to treat it. The current standard of care is to give drugs. An estimated five million children are now being medicated for ADD/ADHD. Even when the drugs don't help, psychiatrists continue to prescribe them warning that if they discontinued, the symptoms could become more severe.

Pediatricians can be just as reckless as psychiatrists in their recommendations in prescribing drugs for ADD/ADHD. The American Academy of Pediatrics just released updated guidelines (October, 2011), recommending the medicating of preschoolers as young as age 4. This, despite the fact that such early use is not approved by the FDA. I'm not saying that medication is never helpful, perhaps in carefully diagnosed children with severe problems who have not responded to parent training and behavioral interventions.This reckless recommendation will continue to escalate the over-diagnosing of children, and the inappropriate prescription of medications to young children.

This story — that if you're behaving or feeling anything other than wonderful in every moment, you could be suffering from a disease and there is a pill that can make it better — is creating a sickly, drug-dependent culture. We are selling drugs in movie trailers, reality TV shows, and Super Bowl spots to a ready and waiting audience who wants to use them to treat all kinds of mythical illnesses. We would eliminate 90% of the "diseases" and psychiatric drugs now being prescribed for tens of millions if we simply prohibited direct-to-consumer advertising by pharmaceutical companies. There are not millions of young children who need to be medicated for these symptoms. There are simply too many parents unable, unwilling, or feeling helpless in changing their kids' behaviors.

I was the second psychiatrist to see 11-year-old Jared after a school psychologist told his parents he needed to be seen by a psychiatrist to treat his Attention Deficit Hyperactivity Disorder (ADHD). Jared was described as a daydreamer, inattentive, and easily distracted. He blurted out answers before the questions were finished, had difficulty waiting his turn for anything, and was a disruptive class clown.

Last year's teacher loved his sense of humor and put up with it, meeting often with his parents to keep things straight. This year's teacher found his behavior intolerable and referred him to the school psychologist who, after a complete evaluation, told the parents that Jared suffered from ADHD and to find a psychiatrist to medicate him. They did, but the standard drugs (Ritalin/Adderall/Vyvanse) didn't help much. They added an antidepressant, which also didn't change things much so they added a new atypical antipsychotic drug. This is the standard of practice in the community today.

Jared slowed down a bit, but he felt like a zombie. He also got fat, so he didn't want to take them anymore. His parents felt terrible watching their son's reaction and came to me because they'd heard I didn't medicate anyone unless absolutely necessary.

I saw the whole family together the first time we met; it included Tom, a 55-year-old information systems manager; Peggy, a 53-year-old stay-at-home mom for the past 12 years; and his eight-year-old sister, Jessica, who had no major problems. Jared bounced from chair to chair in my waiting area, fingering every magazine. When they came into my office, Jared played with the objects on my desk and asked lots of questions but didn't wait for many answers. His father finally said, "Hey Buddy, quiet down, sit here next to me." Jared sat for a short while, and then the scenario was repeated. This time his father told him he had better pay attention, explaining in detail how important this visit was and that we were all trying to help him.

Jessica sat quietly next to her mother holding a doll. Peggy let

Tom do most of the talking. He extolled Jared's virtues; he was a good boy, clever, spontaneous, and funny, and they played and went to ball games together. Tom said that Jared could follow instructions but admitted, in his own time, which led to problems in school. Jared could be redirected if teachers had the time, but with budget cuts and larger classrooms, they simply didn't.

I asked Peggy if there were consequences when Jared didn't listen or perform. She smiled when she said neither she nor Tom was a great enforcer, but if Jared didn't pay attention or complete tasks, he'd get a time out in his room. If it continued, they took away his TV privileges and then his favorite games. In almost every case, the punishments were always short-lived. His charm and wit would suck in one or the other. There was no limit setting, and they could discuss things endlessly until they got angry with each other and then didn't speak for a couple days.

On the other hand, if Jared finished his work and followed the rules, he got lavishly praised and rewarded. If he brought home good grades, he got a triple-scoop ice cream sundae, and if he got good conduct marks, it was worth a new electronic gadget.

After our first visit, I saw his parents alone and Jared alone. We got to know each other, and I slowly weaned him off the medication. His behavior didn't worsen, he lost weight, and if he found things that interested him, he could pay attention too. Jared was interested in the masks and assorted memorabilia that decorate my office. I told him their stories, where I got them, what they meant, and their importance to me. If he interrupted me, I'd respond to his question, but afterward, I'd say I forgot where I was so I'd have to start from the beginning. Consequently, Jared heard the first part of the story a couple of times until he learned to let me finish them. He loved the American Indian artifacts, with their stories of warrior initiations, rituals, and battles (the gorier the better). If he didn't believe me, I'd tell him to look it up. When he was focused, he could read and pay attention.

Tom and Peggy married in their late 30's and both decided to wait a while before having children. When they were ready, they had difficulty in conceiving. With medical attention and fertility drugs, Peggy got pregnant and was 41 when Jared was born. They both knew they were overindulgent and both had trouble enforcing the rules. They discussed things endlessly, which usually ended in days of silence. They felt its impact on their relationship, were ready to look at their problems, and make whatever changes were necessary to help Jared and themselves.

So we talked about...

How To Stop Sh*t Shoveling With Kids

- When you say NO, mean it. Setting limits is an ego corrective experience, and it's important to learn early on that you can't always get what you want.

- Start with this: restore the evening dinner meal as a family ritual. NO computers, cell phones, or texting is allowed at the dinner table! It's a place to talk about the kind of day you had, a problem, or a great thing. Connect at the family level.

- Kids are responsible for their behavior and their actions. Don't get sucked into their blame game about who or what makes them do it.

- There are consequences for not behaving and BE CONSISTENT. If you keep undermining each other and don't follow through with what you say, you'll be shoveling this shit forever. You have a choice – you can raise them, or they will raze you.

- Rewards are good BUT don't over-reward for ordinary expectations because it reinforces the idea that any performance is a great achievement. That's not the standard of excellence by which they will be judged and rewarded in the future. Deep down they know the extravagant praise is bullshit anyway.

- Your kids are not your buddies, at least not yet. What you owe them is your love and commitment to make them competent, to provide them with a strong foundation so that they can later leave that nest and fly alone.

- Go away on weekends or vacations to places without wireless distractions, places where you can be together.

- Raise your kids in community. Surround yourself with family and friends who support you, know you at the soul level, and share your values, because they will be there for you and you will be there for them, no matter what.

Over the next year Jared got off the psychiatric drugs, lost weight, and his schoolwork improved. Tom and Peggy found they could set consistent limits, and they were feeling better about each other. Over the next years, Jared parlayed his computer expertise with his interest in ancient cultures to develop a computer game. In this intergalactic battle, participants joined tribes, practiced initiation rituals, and conquered new frontiers. It was suitably intriguing and bloody to interest a software company in buying his prototype.

Chapter Eight
Stop Your Sh*t Shoveling

Let's be clear. All of us have the capacity to shovel shit. Events happen in our lives that seem to invite habitual behaviors that often make us unhappy. Some of us shovel shit to avoid confrontation, to keep the peace, or to be polite because a higher authority requires it, or we're afraid that if we change, it might make us feel worse than we already do. Whatever triggers the shoveling behavior, the longer we do it, the more we will keep doing it. The cortical connections and biochemistry of the brain react to these shit shoveling triggers almost instantaneously. The more ingrained these patterned responses become, the deeper those embedded brain pathways get.

Here's the good news: the brain has the capacity to reprogram itself. As a species, we have the capacity to create new brain pathways, and it happens when we change our response patterns.

When something happens that triggers your automatic reactions on those well-worn brain paths and old shoveling temptations call, here is how to…

STOP SH*T SHOVELING

Look at your behavior and acknowledge the pain it brings you.

When you feel yourself getting trapped by your old habits, take a break. Create a detour from your ordinary thinking, and change your environment. There are many ways to do it: meditate every day even if it's only five or 10 minutes (maybe find a class at your local YMCA if there's not a Zen meditation center; learn yoga/tai chi/aikido and it'll get you into a different state of mind; run, dance zumba, joining a drum circle, take pictures in the woods, or perform a healing ceremony. Distract yourself.

Now that you've distracted yourself, get out a pencil and a piece of paper. Draw three columns. In the first column write GOALS, and under it, list what you want in your life. The next column is VALUES. Under that, write down your core beliefs, like freedom, justice, health, respect, choice, etc. The last column is titled, IF I PICK UP MY SHOVEL. Under this, next to the goals and values you listed, write a YES or NO if picking up your shovel will help you achieve them.

If you see a lot of NO's, it's time to reach out for some support. Get connected with a professional or support group that strengthens your will and reinforces how you want to come to the world.

Remember, it takes only one step at a time, you'll keep getting stronger, and nobody gets to the Promised Land in a day.

POSTSCRIPT

I'm on the journey with you. Let's stay connected on the healing journey through my Facebook fan page.

http://www.facebook.com/stopshovelingshit

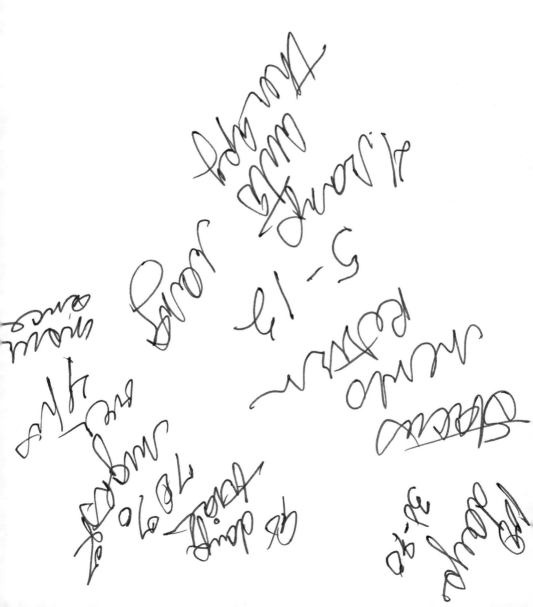

CPSIA information can be obtained at www.ICGtesting.com
Printed in the USA
LVOW10s2156300915

456450LV00025B/669/P